BILSTON, BRADLEY & LADYMOOR

A THIRD SELECTION

RON DAVIES

SUTTON PUBLISHING

Sutton Publishing Limited
Phoenix Mill · Thrupp · Stroud
Gloucestershire · GL5 2BU

First published 2003

Copyright © Ron Davies, 2003

ISBN 0-7509-3089-6

British Library Cataloguing in Publication Data
A catalogue record for this book is available from the
British Library.

Typeset in 10.5/13.5 Photina.
Typesetting and origination by
Sutton Publishing Limited.
Printed and bound in England by
J.H. Haynes & Co. Ltd, Sparkford.

THE BLACK COUNTRY SOCIETY

The Black Country Society is proud to be associated with **Sutton Publishing** of Stroud. In 1994 the society was invited by Sutton Publishing to collaborate in what has proved to be a highly successful publishing partnership, the extension of the *Britain in Old Photographs* series into the Black Country. In this joint venture the Black Country Society has played an important role in establishing and developing a major contribution to the region's photographic archives by encouraging society members to compile books of photographs of the area or town in which they live.

The first book in the Black Country series was *Wednesbury in Old Photographs* by Ian Bott, launched by Lord Archer of Sandwell in November 1994. Since then 55 Black Country titles have been published. The total number of photographs contained in these books is in excess of 11,000, suggesting that the whole collection is probably the largest regional photographic survey of its type in any part of the country to date.

This voluntary society, affiliated to the Civic Trust, was founded in 1967 as a reaction to the trends of the late 1950s and early 1960s. This was a time when the reorganisation of local government was seen as a threat to the identity of individual communities and when, in the name of progress and modernisation, the industrial heritage of the Black Country was in danger of being swept away.

The general aims of the society are to stimulate interest in the past, present and future of the Black Country, and to secure at regional and national levels an accurate understanding and portrayal of what constitutes the Black Country and, wherever possible, to encourage and facilitate the preservation of the Black Country's heritage.

The society, which now has over 2,500 members worldwide, organises a yearly programme of activities. There are six venues in the Black Country where evening meetings are held on a monthly basis from September to April. In the summer months, there are fortnightly guided evening walks in the Black Country and its green borderland, and there is also a full programme of excursions further afield by car. Details of all these activities are to be found on the society's website, **www.blackcountrysociety.co.uk**, and in *The Blackcountryman*, the quarterly magazine that is distributed to all members.

PO Box 71 · Kingswinford · West Midlands DY6 9YN

Title page photograph: Tucked away in a quiet garden spot between the rusting columns on High Street traffic island and Betty's Arch on the Coseley Road traffic island is this old rolling mill. A plaque states: 'It was first installed at the English Electric Company, until it was transferred to Woodstone Rolling Mill, where it was in use from 1976 to 1993.' From here the rolling mill was moved to Bilston for permanent and honourable retirement. (*Author*)

CONTENTS

Glass teapots are fairly rare items. This particular one was produced by the British Heat Resisting Glass Company Ltd, brand name Phoenix, whose works were located in Loxdale Street. The teapot has a delicate look and feel about it, and it took the firm a considerable time to perfect it, only for the works to close soon afterwards, in July–August 1970. Consequently, these particular teapots have now become collectable items. (*Author*)

Here are just a few of the wonderful Compton Hospice volunteers, whose work ranges generally from help in the wards to the various charity shops, even to gardening. Seen here from left to right are Iris Gamble, Alison Littleford, Bernard Howell, Maggie Perry and Chris Bibb. (*Roy Hawthorne*)

INTRODUCTION

T o reiterate a statement from the earlier books on the Bilston, Bradley and Ladymoor area, Bilston is of some antiquity. The Domesday charters state it belonged to the king and comprised two hides of land (approximately 240 acres) and belonged in the Seisdon Hundred. Each Hundred consisted of 100 hides, though Seisdon was one of the long hundreds and comprised 120 hides; one male per hide was selected as a warrior. Staffordshire contained five hundreds, so in case of trouble Staffordshire had command of 600 men at arms.

Bradley, however, only consisted of one hide and belonged in the Offlow Hundred and not to the king but to William, son of Ansculph, Baron of Dudley. The Domesday charters state that Walbert 'holds 1 hide from William in Bradley. Land for 2 ploughs. 4 villagers have 1 plough. Woodland 3 furlongs long and 1 furlong wide. The value was and is 64d. Untan held it, with full jurisdiction. Meadow, 2 acres.'

The Seisdon Hundred today is known as the Seisdon Rural District and the village of that name lies tranquilly about 7 crow miles due west of Bilston. The so-called Hundred House where official law meetings were held is still to be seen and is built of local sandstone, and half of the water mill here once belonged to a certain

Going, going. After dominating the Bilston skyline for twenty-seven years this magnificent feat of engineering is no more. Although some of the early blast furnaces had at least a hundred years of useful pig-iron production, they too went the same way, so today the Black Country does not have a single example of what should have been a fine industrial heritage!

Geoffrey de Bradelea of Bradley in 1227. A former mill on the site is now a private residence that displays a millstone in its front garden.

Bilston's only known watermill formerly stood on the Bilston–Coseley boundary, where Coseley Road and Broadlanes met, until the new toll road crossed the site during the last quarter of the eighteenth century.

But time marches on, and our rural acres have gone. The population in 1780 was a mere 3,000, and by 1949 had risen to 32,720. Heaven knows what the number is today. Most of the open spaces have now been gobbled up by the ever-increasing need for houses. At one time the majority of the population clung to the main shopping area of the town, yet until the 1930s and 1940s Bilston had vast open spaces, albeit pit bank waste. There was the Pink Pool area that stretched from Green Lanes to Stowheath Lane, now mainly covered by the Stowlawn housing estate. The wide open lands of the Lunt were among the first to be estated. Bradley had its Lower Bradley area, whereas Ladymoor with its mile-long winding village had plenty of open land on either side. Its character lay in the slag heaps, its pools and streams, all brimming with wildlife that the others seemed to lack.

What open space remains today is scheduled to become an urban village, stretching from Morrison's superstore across Dudley Street and on through Capponfield to Ladymoor. In doing this it is hoped to open up part of the now ducted Bilston Brook as a focal point. I wonder if they will create a replica water mill there, serving refreshments and with gracious lawns edging down to the stream. One can only dream, but I do look forward to an improved Bilston and locality, just as I have looked back with all the old photographs that have been enshrined within the three volumes which have served to tell some of the story of our Bilston, Bradley and Ladymoor.

This small gathering at the Spring Vale Sports and Social Club in February 2002 was to present a £500 cheque to Compton Hospice fund-raiser, Judy Polkinhorn. The donation was raised at the launch of the second book about Bilston, Bradley and Ladymoor in old photographs. Seen here are Dennis Turner MP, Ron Davies and Judy Polkinhorn. (*Picture by Dave Hamilton, Wolverhampton Express and Star*)

1
Bilston

This rare old photograph by John Price of Bilston shows how Mount Pleasant looked way back in the past. The new Drill Hall is on the left with one cannon showing, then the Theatre Royal, with the Globe Inn on the opposite side of the road.
(Donated by Bill Price)

Before the Town Hall was built in 1872 this half-timbered building, according to John Price in his *Story of Bilston* (p. 31), was used as the Town Public Offices. Since those official days the building has been used for a variety of different purposes. Supposedly in a conservation area the old timber cladding is now falling off; this, combined with the unused and deteriorating Town Hall, leaves this area of the town a shadow of its former self. (*Author*)

Percival's sweets and tobacco shop stood opposite the Town Hall and on the corner of The Orchard. The lady in the doorway is Mrs Nell Percival, and she is seen here in 1919. The photograph was loaned by Nell's daughter, now Mrs Joyce Sinclair. Nell's sister, May, married Sgt Hall of Bilston Police Force in about 1922. (*Joyce Sinclair*)

An old-fashioned wedding scene outside St Leonard's Church, 1930. No bride or bridegroom can be seen, though they were Bob Jones and Violet (née Hughes), but what we do see are three bridesmaids. Only one is named: she is the tall one on the left and is Bob's sister Florence. The best man seen behind the bridesmaids is Bob's brother Bill. Note the cast-iron pillars on either side of the church entrance, appropriately placed on rising cast-iron plinths and topped with urn-like features. They are embossed with the date 1827, along with the name of the architect, Francis Goodwin, who designed the present church. (*Ann Lakin*)

Another scene outside St Leonard's, April 1961. This time it is the turn of the clergy, choir and church officials to pose for the camera. Back row, left to right: Tom Leadbetter, Ken Wilkinson, Frank Hordley, Brian Lockley, Percy Whittle, Granville Bradon, -?-, Jim Bromley, Harry Banner, Bert Wordley. Middle row: -?-, -?-, -?-, -?-, -?-, -?-, David Mears, -?-, -?-, -?-, Mike Lavender, Barry Southall and Mr Alf Skeldon. Front row: Pauline Mears, -?-, -?-, Deaconess Frost, Revd George Shrimpton (Curate), Mr Wellings (Churchwarden), Revd Bernard Jacobs, Mr Roderick (Organist and Choirmaster), Revd David Marsh (Curate), Mr Arthur Henderson (Churchwarden). Note the two pillars still at the church entrance – one of the urns is missing, and today the whole lot is missing, stolen between 14 and 15 September 1999. (*St Leonards Church*)

Violet Homfray takes a stroll along Mount Pleasant in about 1960; it seems that the boy in short trousers is her companion, as it looks as though he is carrying her handbag. On the right of the picture there are three buildings: the first is the police station, the second, with the gable end, has been demolished to make way for a police car park, and the third is the Globe Inn, a popular haunt for the theatricals who performed at the Theatre Royal on the opposite side of the road. (*Harold Humphries*)

A rare royal visit to Bilston took place when the Duke of Kent, as president of the Scout Association, came to unveil a plaque to open the refurbished Scout Hall in Prouds Lane in November 2001. The original hall had been damaged by arsonists twelve months earlier. Back row, left to right: Neil Babb, Ben Lane, Anthony Foster, Kian Hunt, Paul Mehmi. Front row: HRH the Duke of Kent, Ryan Powell, Alex Bradbury, Ryan Jeavon, Ben Jenkins, Adam Lane. (*Picture by Alan Evans, Wolverhampton Express and Star*)

Of the handsome buildings seen here only the smaller manse now remains. The larger building (the Methodist church, Swan Bank) was taken down in the 1960s and replaced by a new but smaller church in 1970. The old building was reputedly the first building in the town to be lit by gas in 1824. In this 1920s scene by the time the photographer had set up, he could be sure of an inquisitive group of bystanders. (*Ron Davies Collection*)

By the year 1963 Bilston Methodist church had amalgamated with other local Methodist churches to form a society. This occasion for the group at Bilston was a circuit rally. A few of those present are, back row, left to right: Lillian Barnett, -?-, -?-, -?-, Alice Clemson, Eva Bailey, Mary Bailey, N. Wilkinson, -?-, -?-, -?-, -?-. Middle row: Miss Heavens, -?-, -?-, -?-. Front row: -?-, -?-, -?-, -?-, Mrs Rogers with her daughter Betty, Hilda Lee, -?-, -?-, -?-, -?-. (*N. Wilkinson*)

The old Bilston Holy Trinity School in Queen Street, seen in 1990, now remains unused and boarded up after serving its little community for the best part of ninety years. The timbered annexe seen at the end of the school building was always a special feature here, and served as an extra schoolroom. (*Author*)

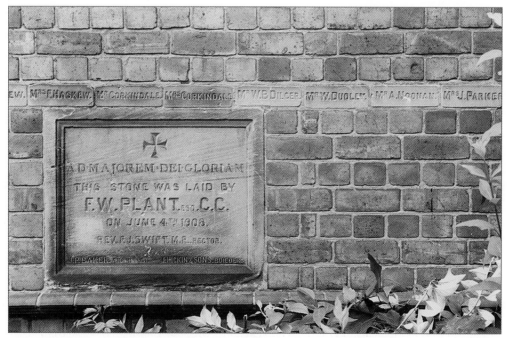

One of the features of the school building is a well-preserved date-stone. Even more interesting are the named bricks seen topping the date-stone; no doubt these are the people who helped to finance the building of the school. The Latin states AD MAJOREM DEI GLORIAM – TO THE GREATER GLORY OF GOD. (*Author*)

Some of the football sporting scholars of the Holy Trinity School pose proudly for this 1921/2 picture. Back row, left to right: E. Hardwick, J. Cox, J. Knight, W. Walters, E. Roberts, J. Curley. Front row: T. Flanagan, A. Fellows, S. Roberts, B. Harris, T. Taffano. (*Joe Knight*)

When the world moved at a more leisurely pace. This scene from the early 1920s shows Mr Bill Price at his job as a carter. The haulier's business belonged to Mr J. Poulton of Oxford Street, so the waste scene, seen in the background, would not have been far removed from Oxford Street. It is a wonderful study of a working horse in full harness and the type of cart last seen in the area in about 1960. (*Joe Knight*)

The same carter, Mr Bill Price, but a different horse, cart and scene, this time in the 1930s. The tank presumably contained lamp oil, which was still widely used for household illumination, and the scene is believed to be outside Mr Poulton's shop in Oxford Street. (*Joe Knight*)

Another family of shopkeepers in Oxford Street were the Billingsleys who dealt in green-grocery. Here, *c.* 1920, we see in the back row, left to right: Jack Heming, -?-, Jack Robinson, -?-. Front row: Edie, Pamela, Clara and Mary Billingsley. (*John Aston, Darlaston, donated by Joe Knight*)

St Mary's Church, Oxford Street, as it looks today. It was erected in 1830 in a Gothic style. (*Author*)

This interior of St Mary's dates back to 1910, and looks very different from today. The church appears to have family pews, and the lighting system looks very much as though it has gas or early electricity. The Gothic interior appears to be in the Perpendicular style. (*Joe Knight*)

Whatever one needs in the way of home furnishings, here at Bilston at least the name Cole springs to mind for quality and a fair price. It all started way back in 1921 when Bill Cole, pictured here in the mid-1960s, set up a yard on the Great Bridge Road and over the years filled it with household bric-à-brac ranging from timber to cement and from cookers to toilets, with the added attraction of a menagerie of animals from all over the world. Bill loved animals; he also loved people, especially if they bought something! He could be brusque and he stood for no nonsense. Some would try it on but not a second time. Bill was a great character, the likes of whom we shall never see again. (*Cole's Furnishers*)

This is Bill Cole's ramshackle yard, *c.* 1965. There was no real order here but Bill knew where everything was – one couldn't catch him out. Above all, he was a good businessman. (*Cole's Furnishers*)

This is a modern view of Bilston Library in Mount Pleasant. The library also serves as a museum and art gallery; earlier the building had been the Bilston Girls' High School. It is a rather modern building put up in about 1905, and built on the site of a much older one of *c.* 1818, then the home of the Brueton family who, among other businesses, were lock manufacturers. (*Author*)

Housed in the library is this set of chairs formerly used by the various mayors of the town. The chair in the centre is emblazoned with the Bilston coat of arms, designed by W.J. Kape, who was principal of the Art and Technical College in Mount Pleasant during the 1930s. The chairs were made by the cabinet-making firm of Eccleston, who had their workshops where the tile showrooms now are on the Millfield Road. (*Author*)

This lovely study of a proud little girl shows Miss Rosemary Price as she was in Form 1 at the Bilston Girls' High School in 1927. That year she gained a first-class badge for her work, and she penned a little poem, as most young pupils were encouraged to do: this was her contribution.

My Pets

I have a little rabbit
And he lives in his hutch;
I play with him all day,
And I like him very much.

I have a little kitten,
And she runs about the house;
Once I heard her squeaking,
For she had caught a mouse.

But best of all are pigeons,
For I love to hear them coo,
When it's early in the morning,
And I'm awake too.

As Mrs Emerson, she lived at the Buttery in Finchfield, Wolverhampton, a lovely half-timbered Jacobean house which formerly stood in Shifnal, Shropshire. (*A Bennet Clark photograph donated by Judy Wilson*)

A more recent pose, or rather two poses, *c.* 1948. They show Miss Ann Jones (now Mrs Ann Lakin) happy to be seen in both her regular high school uniform and the other, looking very smart, in full uniform. It really was an excellent high school, and it is sad that it all had to come to an end. (*Ann Lakin*)

This happy scene features some of the girls of Brueton House Girls' High School, *c.* 1920–1. The only girl who can be identified here is Lillian Hughes; she is seen directly in front of the teacher. (*Ann Lakin*)

This is a large gathering of high school girls and their families for some special occasion, said to have been held in Hickman Park during the 1920s or '30s. There were not many salubrious open spaces around at that time, but this is clearly one of them. Stowheath Park, situated on the Wolverhampton side of the Bilston–Wolverhampton border, may well have fitted the occasion, but Hickman Park was more convenient, especially where young children were concerned. (*Ann Lakin*)

This delightful group of dancing fairies has a date of 1920. After all these years only one face is known, that of Violet Hughes, then simply known as Tiny; she is seen peeping from the back right, with beads on her arm. This is probably a school photograph, and as she at that time lived in Oxford Street, the likeliest local school would have been Frazer Street (Etheridge) School. (*Ann Lakin*)

The next few photographs are just a few of the beautiful Bilston enamels that were once housed in the museum section at Bilston Library. This one is probably a patch box; the patches they held were used to hide skin sores that were common in the eighteenth century. The collection was transferred to Bantock House Museum when Bilston was taken over by Wolverhampton in about 1966, and from there, it is said, they were subsequently lost. (*Derek Simpkiss*)

Candlesticks such as these were once popular items to be fashioned by the enamellers. They were practical as well as decorative, and this pair had a lovely green opaque lustre. (*Derek Simpkiss*)

Items such as this must have been something quite special, for here we have three small pots set beautifully upon a striking decorated tray. (*Derek Simpkiss*)

This is a simple but wonderfully decorated box, and quite a valuable item. The museum also held beautiful specimens of Bilston pottery, the likes of which one never sees on the *Antiques Road Show*. (*Derek Simpkiss*)

This pleasant Tudor-style building is next to the Bilston Library and serves the Conservative members of the community. It was formerly the home of the Wood family, who brought so much entertainment to the town in the way of cinema during the early years of the last century. The flag commemorates the Queen's Golden Jubilee in 2002. (*Author*)

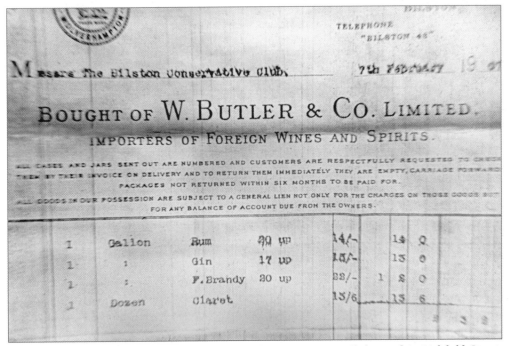

This is an old bill dating back to 1907, when the Conservative Club stood in Lichfield Street. Butler's Brewery held sway in the town for many years, until the 1960s. (*Jack Braddock*)

A turn of the century view of Church Street, showing on the corner of Homer's Fold, with the awning, what was popularly known as the Fancy Draper, while next door found grocers K. & S. Pratt. The buildings had been half-timbered but the fashion of the day saw the whole lot stuccoed over. It is believed that a fire here in the 1920s damaged most of the frontages. (*The Bilston Almanac*)

This is more or less the same view as that above, but with modern façades. This shot dates from before the town was pedestrianised; mobile phones have now taken over James Baker shoes and the MEB office showroom is now an Argos Catalogue store. (*Author*)

A trolley-bus scene looking down Church Street, *c.* 1960. This was Bilston town still at its best, with a good old-fashioned Woolworths on the right and Burton's Tailors on the left, over which there was a dance hall popular with lovers of ballroom dancing. (*Ron Davies Collection*)

The London School of Ballroom Dancing (situated over Burton's Tailors in Church Street and run by teachers Jimmy and Sylvia Sharpe) take a trip to Dingle Lake, near Bridgnorth, *c.* 1953. Here members pose happily alongside the coach. Left to right: -?-, -?-, -?-, Bill Marsh, Ron Hammersley, Ray Hammersley, -?-, -?-, Ivor Palmer, Alan Stanley, Bernard ?, Gordon Everton, Jean Everton, -?-, -?-, Des Price, Edna Price, -?-, Gerald Marsden, -?-, Margaret Hale, Sylvia Sharpe, -?-, Jimmy Sharpe, -?-, Gwen Sutton, Doreen Marsden, Doreen Bird, Verna Hammersley, -?-, Fran Beddows, Mrs Bird, Jim Beddows, -?-, Mr Bird. The children are the daughters of Jim and Fran Beddows. (*Ivor Palmer*)

In 1328 a Charter of Freedom from tolls as a market town was given. In 1824 a public market was established by Act of Parliament. This market was held in Church Street, and the one shown here with its commanding classical façade was opened in about 1892 by Sir Alfred Hickman. It became a mecca for people from miles around, as is the present market; old habits die hard. (*Ron Davies Collection*)

The first stall through the left doorway of the market was a wet fish counter, long served by Mr Gerry Sands and his daughter Penny. Both of them are seen here in about 1968; their speciality was shellfish which attracted many regular customers. (*Derek Simpkiss*)

The fish business still carries on, though now in the new market place, through Gerry's son Roger and his daughter Cassie, continuing the father and daughter tradition. The stall still boasts perhaps the widest selection of both wet and shellfish in the town. (*Author*)

Still with the old market, here's nostalgia in the way of 78 rpm records, *c.* 1950. They did as brisk a trade then as they do now with state-of-the-art CDs. (*Derek Simpkiss*)

Not only did the old timber-framed buildings suffer, but also their Georgian and Victorian successors. These particular buildings, Rose Villas, in Broad Street, were only saved in the nick of time by the then Bilston Conservation Association, as being the only remaining domestic Victorian Gothic architecture left in the town. Here they are being restored in the early 1980s. (*Author*)

A delightful spot in days gone by at Hickman Park, late 1930s. The fountain was wonderfully ornate in cast-iron and was well used; the water was Bilston's own, pumped from the Bratch at Wombourne. In the background on the right one can make out the bandstand. All of this has now gone; so much has been lost from this lovely park gifted to the town in 1911 by the Hickman family. The grounds, however, are very well kept and the park is still a pleasure to walk around. (*Ron Davies Collection*)

Until about 1970 Thompson Street, off High Street, was a typical old dwelling area, and with its neighbouring Hartshorn Street was possibly the last of the old terraces to succumb to the Slum Clearance Act. Most were in better order than other slum areas and in their day were much-sought-after residences, but lack of the modern facilities that we take for granted today finally ensured their demise. (*Ron Davies Collection*)

Formerly standing in High Street, next to Thompson Street, this building with very simple classical features served as a Primitive Methodist church. Built in 1841, it saw its last service in December 1962. Many local businessfolk formed part of its congregation, including Bilston's first mayor, Alderman Herbert Beach, who besides being the organist was also a Sunday School teacher. This view dates from the early 1960s. (*Bob Hampton*)

This tree-lined scene, better known in days past as Railway Drive, led to Bilston railway station (once situated just to the left of the picture), *c.* 1975. When visitors and businesspeople came to the town, it gave a good impression, especially with the Pipe Hall Hotel dominating the Drive. There were some impressive houses too, just seen on the right in the background. The Belfast roof-type buildings, also seen on the right, were the warehouses of Mr Ikey Brown, who was a leading Bilston wallpaper merchant. The Black Country Route now crosses the scene. (*Author*)

At one time the Bilston fire station stood in Market Street next to the outdoor market, more or less where the market is today. This was the type of engine in use in the second half of the 1960s. (*Ron Davies*)

Looking like a bomb-site, this is part of the new Black Country Route being constructed in the Prosser Street area, *c.* 1990. Sankey's offices can be seen to the right, and the last of the council houses in Stonefield Walk in the distant left, while the footbridge over the whole is in the process of being built. (*Author*)

Friday 21 July 1995 saw the official opening of the Black Country Route by Neil Kinnock MEP. Mr Kinnock is seen driving a classic Sunbeam car, made in Wolverhampton; with him in the front is Councillor Norman Davies, with Councillor Trudy Bowen and Dennis Turner MP in the back. At a cost of £110 million the 4½ mile route runs from the Birmingham New Road at Deepfields, Coseley, to join Junction 10 of the M6 at Bentley. (*Wolverhampton Express and Star*)

The Stonefield sports field was formerly the site of Stonefield furnace and ironworks, as seen here, *c.* 1870. They were the works of Messrs Chambers and Sankey, who also had mills and twenty puddling furnaces here. This is where Joseph Sankey could take complete control of the special irons he needed for his many products. Note the GWR (OWWR) embankment in the background. (*Samuel Griffiths*)

This is how the Stonefield sports site looked twenty-five years ago, with the Elisabeth towering in the background about a mile distant, just where the car is seen on the old Bilston to Coseley Way. This was the last of the shallow coal seams in the area; it was where colonies of crickets enjoyed year-round warmth. The smell was far from pleasant, but surprisingly there was a small allotment garden close by. (*Author*)

The sports field site as it looks today, still with the line of the old railway in evidence. (*Author*)

A sad picture of neglect, this is the once-proud Stonefield school built in about 1905. In its time it educated a very large percentage of the town's youth, from tots to teenagers. Parts of the school are still in use, but come under such names as Colton Hills or Parkfields, as it is felt the name Stonefield is now one to be avoided. The road, or old right of way, seen alongside the school here, is part of the one that in past days led into the Highfields area of Coseley. (*Author*)

In 1950 the Stonefield sports field was honoured by the presence of at least two Wolverhampton Wanderers star footballers, who came to play a friendly cricket match against the local Sankey's team. Here we see Billy Wright with Bill Shorthouse, who dominates the picture. In the background to the right is the GWR embankment, in the left background is an old slag heap, while further back Perry's Foundry in Bradley can be seen. (*Maisie Evans*)

Here Billy Wright and company take a rest – but they are quite happy to pose for the camera. (*Maisie Evans*)

Standing cheek by jowl alongside the Black Country Route at Prosser Street lies the old Stonefield School. Here is a junior school class of ten-year-olds, *c.* 1945. Back row, left to right: -?-, -?-, -?-, Clifford Sirrett, Reggie Carter, -?-, -?-, Leslie Bates, -?-, -?-, ? Hutt, Freda Williams and Hazel Poole. Front row: Betty Franklin, Joan Raybone, Maisie Southall, June Smart, -?-, -?-, -?-, Betty Bird, -?-, Cissy Fullwood. (*Maisie Evans*)

These girls from the same junior class, seen working as a Country Dance team are, from left to right: Freda Williams, Hazel Poole, Maisie Southall, Joan Raybone, Cissy Fullwood, -?-. (*Maisie Evans*)

The Hand and Bottle Inn, seen here in about 1965, was one of four pubs to be found in Wolverhampton Street. All were swept away during the slum clearance mainly in the 1970s and '80s. This particular pub stood between the Hand and Keys and the Barrel. (*Black Country Society*)

This sketch by Andrew Barnett shows the old stonemason's building in Hickman's Yard, Millfields Road, now in the Black Country Living Museum. The huge slab of carboniferous limestone was hewn out of the local stone quarry early in the twentieth century. It measured 13ft 4in in length and about 2 ft square, and was still in evidence until 1990. This drawing is from the mid-1920s. (*Andrew Barnett*)

Looking east from the old stone building towards High Street, *c.* 1960. The garage site, Wallet and Rowley, seen on the left, is still with us, though long under other managements, and the BP sign on the right denotes Hazeldine's garage. By the late 1980s this scene had completely disappeared. (*Harry Eccleston*)

Adjacent to the stonemasons' building stood the West Midland Refining Co. Ltd, or the cupola melting furnace, known by the locals as the Pop Bottle. Here an advert displays the various types of special irons produced for a wide variety of uses in the iron trades. (*A Staffordshire Handbook*)

This large gathering shows but a few of the employees who worked at the E.N. Wright works at Millfields. The occasion was the retirement of Mr E.N. Wright, and these were the elite workers who maintained the vast Spring Vale and other steelworks. Back row, left to right: -?-, -?-, -?-, Ray Walters, -?-, -?-, -?-, -?-, Li Sims, -?-, -?-, -?-, -?-. Seventh row: -?-, -?-, Jack Powell, Arthur Bagley, Alan Shaw, Ron Davies, Al Hollinshead, -?-, -?-, -?-, -?-. Sixth row: Jack Doughty, Harry Johnson, Eric Gill, -?-, Bill Yates, Ted Lockett, -?--?-, Geoff Bird, Jean Page, Joyce Jones. Fifth row: Jack (Sandy) Powell, Charlie Hale, -?-, Ivan Beech, Herbert Griffiths, -?-, Ken Stanley, -?-, -?-, -?-, Jill Brough, Jim Brough. Fourth row: Bill Lloyd, Jack Perks, George Bates, Selwyn Jones, Harold Jones, -?-, -?-, Reg Brant, -?-, -?-, -?-. Third row: -?-, -?-, Alan Bird, Ben Crowther Harry New, Jim Elwell, Dick Ball, Ted Lockett Sr, -?-, -?-, -?-. Second row: Bill Huntbatch, Jim Biddle, Sid Jones, -?-, -?-, Tom Fellows, -?-, -?-. Front row: George Jones, -?-, Ray Stanley, -?-, Arthur Bryan, Harry Jones Ernie Rollason, Bill Cadman, Mo Holden, -?-. Standing on the left: Joe Jones, -?-, -?-, Len Mountford Standing on the right: -?-, Bill Cox, Jim Perks, Alf Hollyhead, Cyril Evans, -?-, Cyril Dams, Mrs Brenda Wright, E.N. Wright, Mr Reginald Wright, -?-, -?-, -?-, Jack Askin, -?-, -?-, -?-, -?-, -?-, -?-. *(Harry Johnson)*

A study in watercolour by Robert Baker of Alfred Hickman's furnaces, *c.* 1930. The works at that time were known as the Hot Holes.

These engines supplied the power for the whole works, and those nearest the camera were furnace-blowing engines, *c.* 1950. One rarely had the opportunity to see into this department. (*Derek Simpkiss*)

Old hand Tom Simpkiss is seen here attending to the diesel engines that drove the works generators, *c.* 1950. (*Derek Simpkiss*)

This huge 1,000 hp gas engine was the first to be installed at the Alfred Hickman works, seen in about 1950. The steady rhythm of the engines combined with all the other industrial sounds to form a passive throb that strangers found intrusive but which locals took for granted like a mother's heartbeat. (*Derek Simpkiss*)

These two views of the Elisabeth show the vast complexity of steel fabrication needed to work this huge enterprise, an evolution that took 200 years from the first stone-bodied furnaces built on the site. The process for even more efficient furnaces is still continuing, albeit elsewhere. These photographs date from the 1970s.
(*Harry Eccleston*)

No flashing lights or sirens blaring on this vehicle as it carried injured workers post-haste to the Royal Hospital. Yes, this was the works ambulance used during the Hickman era. (*Steelworks News, No. 54, L. McGowan*)

Like the main-line locomotives, the steelworks locos too had pet names. This narrow-gauge side tanker was *Doll* and worked in the melting shop; she was eventually retired to the Leighton Buzzard Railway. She had a sister loco, *Gertrude*, but her fate is unknown. (*Steelworks News, No. 54, L. McGowan*)

Steam lorries were very much in evidence at the steelworks, at the Tarmac company and around the local area during the early twentieth century. Most were made by a firm known as Sentinel, and they were splendid workhorses; note the solid tyres of the era. A tray slung underneath the engine caught the small spent coal ashes or gleeds, as they were locally known. Often they spilled over the sides and smokers used them to light up. (*Derek Simpkiss*)

The same lorry in the works competing with horse and cart, in this case removing rubbish, 1920s. (*Steelworks News, No. 54, L. McGowan*)

Enjoying an after-dinner pint at the Spring Vale Social Centre, this group of Stewarts and Lloyds Welfare Council committee members posing for the cameraman in 1960–1 are, back row, left to right: Tom Pitt, Reg Brant, Harry Johnson, Ron Topping, -?-, -?-. Second row: J. Round, Bob Morrell, Arthur Dyke, Frank Davidson, Bill Law, Sam Jarvis, Philip Shee. Front row: Arthur Barwell, Charlie Turley, Ben Cashmore, Bill Fieldhouse, -?-. (*Margaret Hampton*)

Employees at the steelworks were numerous and the Spring Vale Social Centre catered for every recreational taste. There was always something going on, and little has changed over the years. Seen here are the Spring Vale winning bowls team for 1976. Standing, left to right: Maurice Jones, Leonard Hull, Jeff Bamford. Sitting: Keith Dodd, Harry Johnson, John Pugh, Arthur Causer. (*Donated by Harry Johnson*)

An earlier bowling K/O team from 1975, with many of the same stalwarts appearing, were, back row, left to right: Jeff Bamford, T. Reynolds, E. Hobbs. Sitting: Maurice Jones, Harry Johnson, Arthur Causer. (*Donated by Harry Johnson*)

The football teams did well too. Here is a happy winning team posing after their 1964/65 success. The back row includes J. Timmins, K. Bryan, H. Wells, K. Brazier and D. Philpot. Front row: Harry Johnson (Chairman), B. Higgins, A. Rollason, B. Priest, F. Sellick, A. Cross, F. Jarman (Secretary), -?-, -?-. (*Donated by Harry Johnson*)

Cricket has always been a top sport with the Social Club members. These happy inter-department winners for 1970 are, back row, left to right: W. Smart, D. Fletcher, S. Campbell, T. Sims, J. Clark, H. Johnson, Ernie Evans, L. Salmon. Sitting: A.R. Thomas, M. Jones, A. Rollason (Captain), A. Causer, J. Bamford. (*Donated by Harry Johnson*)

This cricket team goes back to 1947, which shows that cricket played on the Spring Vale sports ground was just as popular then. Back row, left to right: Alec Robinson, Tom Bate, Eric Emerson, Arthur Summers, Tom Roberts, Gordon Stokes, Reg Astley, -?-. Front row: -?-, -?-, Arthur Jones, Cliff Sutcliffe, Jack Ramsden, -?-, Jim Moore, Philip Shee, -?-. (*Judy Wilson*)

The Spring Vale cricket teams also played many away games and Ventnor on the Isle of Wight was always a popular venue. This 1950 photograph features, back row, left to right: Jim Moore, Jack Mitton, Arthur Summer, -?-, Jack Mitton, Jr, -?-, Eric Emerson, Gordon Stokes, -?-, -?-. Centre row: -?-, Reg Astley, Jack Ramsden, -?-, Tom Sutcliffe, Arthur Jones. Front row: Noel Willis, -?-, -?-. (*Judy Wilson*)

Here we have the same team, posing this time with their wives, children and a pet pekinese. The Isle of Wight trip was always a good excuse for a holiday. (*Judy Wilson*)

Another Isle of Wight picture, this time in 1951. The team is again seen with families and friends. Back row, left to right: -?-, -?-, -?-, Tom Sutcliffe, -?-, -?-, John Emerson, Arthur Summers, Eric Emerson, -?-, -?-, -?-. Third row: Lilian Jones, -?-, -?-, -?-, Mrs Ramsden, Jack Ramsden, Mrs Stokes, Gordon Stokes, Mrs Moore, Jim Moore, -?-, -?-. Second row: Mrs John Emerson, -?-, Edna Emerson, Arthur Groves, -?-, Reg Astley, Pat Ramsden, Arthur Jones, -?-, -?-. Front row: Judy Wilson (née Emerson), -?-, -?-, -?-, -?-, -?-, -?-. (*Judy Wilson*)

Looking like something from outer space, this monster rock weighing many tonnes was one of the surprise finds during the early opencast excavations in the late 1980s, but it became a problem. British Coal's attempts to shatter it by drilling and explosives failed to budge it, so it was later allowed to fall some 200 ft to the bottom of the works. Undoubtedly this was the hearth of a former furnace that had hardened or cyrstallised over the many years of working. What a shame it could not have been saved as a local point of interest. (*Author*)

This is how the rock ended up, at the bottom of the opencast works. (*British Coal*)

Here is opencast site surveyor Paul Tomlinson with amateur geologist Andrew Barnett in front of a backdrop seam of 'brooch' coal, so called because once this seam was broached, miners knew the next seam encountered was the fabulous so-called 30 ft seam. Brooch coal was a most favoured house coal and was generally about 6 ft thick. Andrew with hammer in hand searched for special ironstone nodules that might yield some creature trapped inside, but this never happened. Time here was the main factor, for one was never allowed to be without supervision. (*Author*)

Down on the bed of thick coal, diggers claw hungrily at the yielding coal. Some 360,000 tons of high-grade coal was extracted this way. Once the thick coal was extracted the deeper coals, heathen, new mine, bottom coal, etc., had to be left owing to the relatively small area allowed to dig, and about 200 ft was the limit allowed. (*Author*)

Small rivers were encountered during this huge dig and needed as many as six pumps to stop the site flooding. Generally the waters were black from the coal seams; this one stream, however, seen oozing from beneath the carboniferous limestone beds (Bilston stone) ran orange like the rusty brooks of old. Though looking rusty it was actually crystal clear, but its taste was quite bitter with various minerals, especially iron oxides. This is why the area was known as Spring Vale. (*Author*)

This was one of the giant earth removers employed on the site. (*Author*)

The insignificant-looking black line trapped between fireclay deposits was the first coal seam the miners of old encountered. As it was only 2 ft thick it was unprofitable to work, but it proved a godsend for the shallow pit workers during the 1920s coal strikes, as it lay generally quite close to the surface. (*Author*)

When the 2 ft coal seam was exposed during the opencast workings, it showed quite a goodly lump of coal. (*Author*)

A rare seam noticed during excavations was the marine band, or so-called non-marine band, created during various fluctuating sea levels that left behind bands of mussel bi-valve type creatures (*Carbonicola*), of which a few are seen here. (*Author*)

A more common survivor from the past are the horsetails. Here we see, on the left, a present-day species, and on the right a fossil horsetail (*Calamites*) found on the opencast site. (*Author*)

Another species to survive until the present day is the maidenhair tree, or Ginkgo. Here both the old and the present species are seen; the fossilised one was found in an ironstone nodule on the site here. (*Author*)

Here is a long-forgotten Spring Vale slag heap in the 1920s, gobbled up no doubt by the nearby Tarmac works. Most of the slag heaps had been worked out by the 1950s. Note the ladles and ladle carriages stockpiled on the site. (*Derek Simpkiss*)

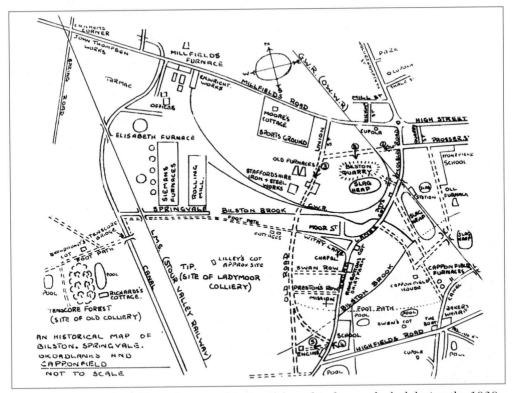

The map gives an idea of how the area of Spring Vale and Ladymoor looked during the 1930s. It is an area that is virtually without any photographic evidence other than of the great steelworks, so one has to rely on memory sketches or else all would be lost. The new Black Country Route now follows the old path that led from Coseley Road to Birmingham New Road, and no doubt it is still remembered by the older generation. (*Author*)

This view looks west from Prosser Street, and shows mainly the Great Western Railway line. The rough foreground was a pit waste area known as the Colliery. The bridge carrying the railway was almost tunnel-like, as there were at least twelve tracks here, some for the steelworks, some for maintenance and some for the goods yard for local businesses. On the other side of the railway large overhead buckets plied to and fro, carrying slag for the Tarmac company, with netting stretched across the path to stop slag falling on pedestrians. To the left of that scene lay the Bilston stone quarries, and the steelworks are seen in the background. (*Author*)

This is just a section of a once large stone quarry, long since disused. By the 1920s the quarry had matured into a green and flowery area much loved by local children. The background shows a huge mound of slag dumped by the Tarmac company, around which a road spiralled that was busy with steam lorries. Local men were employed to break up the slag with sledgehammers. During the war years prisoners of war also helped in this task, their camp being close to Union Street. (*Author*)

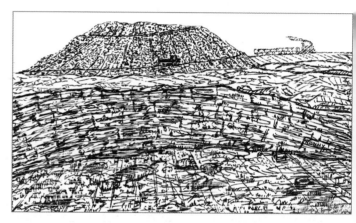

From the quarry to Union Street and the continuing old road into Coseley, the area lay rough with the remains of the former South Staffordshire Ironworks. This area had been held by Sir Alfred Hickman since 1880, and along the road he had constructed this huge building that contained monstrous machinery set upon massive concrete foundations. Phosphorous slag (a by-product of the Bessemer basic steel process) was crushed to form basic slag, a very useful fertiliser. The corrugated steel building seen opposite housed a small locomotive, unused for decades. A gap between the padlocked doors showed that it had a tall chimney with a crown on top. It was set upon a narrow gauge rail track, perhaps no wider than 2 ft, and in its day it plied to and from the Ladymoor coalfields supplying coal to the South Staffordshire Ironworks. (*Author*)

2

Bradley

In the early years of the twentieth century, the Cali Works in Greenway Road was among the foremost ironworks and foundries in the locality. The works probably took its name from the nearby California Inn, in Hatton Street. Here some of the moulders proudly stand with a melting pot at their feet. The picture must date from about 1918. (*Margaret Hampton*)

Bradley 1st Scout and Guide Band parading along Chapel Street on their way to Bradley, *c.* 1968. Seen on the far left is Ann Wood, then Scout Leader Alf Hyate. Nearest in the front row is Dean Harriman, and mace bearer Cheryl ?. (*Derek Wood*)

This time we see Bradley Wulfrun Band marching up Loxdale Street, again towards Bradley, the occasion being Chapel Street's anniversary, 1986–7. (*Derek Wood*)

This elegant pose from 1897 shows John Henry Rolfe of Hatton Street with his wife Ellen and daughter Rosanna. John was a boatman for most of his working life but eventually found work at the Cali. (*Gary Woodberry*)

Still with the same family, but the girl Rosanna seen above is now Mrs Stevens with her own little brood. Left to right we have, John Thomas, Rosanna, Irene and Letty, *c.* 1927. (*Gary Woodberry*)

Local character Tom Perrins prepares for one of his noted walks, the occasion being the Bradley Marathon, *c.* 1960. There were always plenty of runners but only one walker – and that was Tom Perrins. Here in the yard of the Navigation Inn, Salop Street, Tom does a bit of preparing, all very serious. Onlookers are setting their watches. Here among others are, from left to right, Councillor Walter Hughes (grey-haired wearing spectacles), -?-, -?-, Brian Jones (local special constable), with Tom in the centre. Note the spire of St Martin's Church in the background. (*Derek Wood*)

An old scene in Salop Street shows Mary George holding baby son Derek in her arms. The little girl in front is also Mary George, now Mary Brown. The house was no, 21, the year 1934. (*Annette Beaton*)

The Georges were soon to keep the White Hart public house in Salop Street, where they were to stay for many years. This is little Derek, now at two or three years of age, posing in the back yard of the White Hart, 1936. (*Annette Beaton*)

A domestic scene being enjoyed during a lull in Christmas day trading at the White Hart, 1961. Left to right we see Steven Brown (grandson), Arthur George with Topsy the dog, and Derek George, with Rosina George (née Callaghan) in front. (*Annette Beaton*)

These two gentlemen are Mr George Sankey and Mr Luther Greenway, on the occasion of the opening of the Greenway playing field, September 1930. Mr Greenway is on the right. Note his 1930s-style hearing aid. The two men were neighbours in industry at Bankfield and Greenway Road. (*Joan Moseley*)

In order to establish a Bradley Senior Citizens' Centre, many fund-raising events were organised. One of the events for this cause which took place on the Greenway playing field was go-kart racing, which everyone seems to be enjoying here in 1970. (*Derek Wood*)

No carnival is complete without a Carnival Queen, and here posing graciously in 1970 is Miss Maureen Price of Bradley. (*Derek Wood*)

The Carnival Queen poses with her attendants, with proud dad Bill Price looking on. (*Derek Wood*)

The drummers of Bradley 1st Scout Band lead the 1967 Bradley Carnival parade along Highfield Road. In the background on the left can be seen the Prince of Wales public house, now a corner supermarket. The chimney stack and factory roofs are the works of the British Bath, now a small residential estate, and on the right is Hughes' furniture store; at the time of writing it lies vacant. Band personnel noted are, in the left line, Alan Webb, Robert Cooper, Martin Sands and Bryn Jones; in the centre line, mace-bearer Alan Richards and Geoff Vaughan, and on the right is John Grinsell – and look! a Rolls-Royce. (*Derek Wood*)

Still with the 1967 Bradley Carnival, here's what one might call a boatload of trouble – where on earth did the boat come from? (It seems it was loaned by the local police!) The theme is castaways on a tropical shore, with pretty maidens at hand, though all are Bradley boys and girls. The carnival reached Wolverhampton Street, Bilston, where this scene was captured by an *Express and Star* photographer. In the picture area, from left to right, back row: Dawn Parkinson, Lil Reynolds, Becky Gripton (née Perks). The girls in the grass skirts are Dawn Gripton, Maxine Gripton, -?-. The castaways are Darren Parkinson, Ron Reynolds, -?-. (*Donated by Becky Gripton*)

Shields were to be won for the best or most original carnival scenes. There was always a lot of competition and Bradley was pleased to win this one; all those involved are named on the shield. On the left are M.J. Yeomans, A. Hopley, D. Westwood, S. Moriarty, K. Gamble, D. Whitehouse, D. Evans, J. Finch, D. Reynolds, and S. Vickers. On the right are S. Hayward, S. Hayward, A. Lewis, P. Lewis, P. Rudge, G. Mills, G. Archer, J. Jones. (*Shield, Becky Gripton, photo Author*)

The late Sedgley historian Mr Andrew Barnett contemplates a boundary post located in Highfield Road, Bradley, with the initial 'B' for either Bilston or Bradley on one side and 'S' for Sedgley on the other. It being situated outside certain premises often caused confusion for the occupants, either for voting or the payment of rates, and if a child was born in a particular room of the house it could result in the child being registered either in Dudley or in Wolverhampton. (*Author*)

One of the first sights of St Martin's Church was the foundation stone, laid by Miss Apollonia Baldwin whose family, the industrial Baldwins, were responsible for building the church. Unfortunately Apollonia died before the church was consecrated in 1868. (*Author*)

One of the last sights of the church, shown here, was the taking down of the spire in 1978, little more than 100 years after it was built. (*Author*)

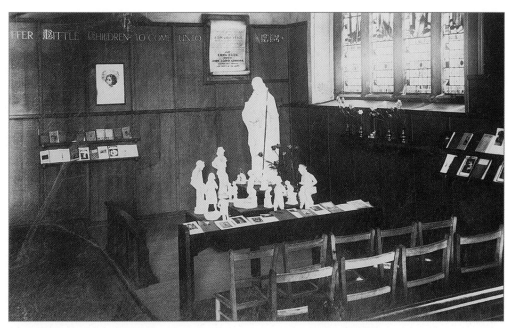

This quiet corner of St Martin's was known as the Lady Chapel or Children's Corner. (*Eileen Reynolds*)

Bazaars were once popular events at St Martin's. Seen here enjoying a game of roll-a-penny in 1958 are, from left to right, Edith Hazlehurst, Iris and Len Hazlehurst and their daughter Jean. (*Iris Hazlehurst*)

One of St Martin's events of 1956 was a visit from the Bishop of Accra (then the Gold Coast, now Ghana). Here the Revd E.A. Dentith welcomes him at Wolverhampton station along with two leading church members, Mr Harry Crane (left) and Mr Hartill. (*Derek Wood*)

By 1958 Mr Dentith had moved to a living on Jersey. Here church members pay him a visit; they are, from left to right, Ann Wood (née Neale), Derek Wood, John Grinsell, and June McLachlan (née Grinsell). (*Derek Wood*)

The Revd E.A. Dentith was happy to
return to Bradley, this time to open
the Bradley Gala or carnival in 1967.
(*Derek Wood*)

Here Mr Dentith is seen addressing the crowd on this special 1967 carnival day taking place on
the Greenway playing field, with the vicar of the day, the Revd A.W. Moseley, and their wives in
attendance. Councillor Dennis Turner is on the extreme right of the picture. (*Derek Wood*)

This is the present vicar of St Martin's, the Revd R. Walker, being filmed for a South Wales TV programme, for our intrepid vicar and his wife Celia like nothing more than taking to the skies during visits to the Gower Peninsula and para-gliding, hence the great interest. Another adventurous feature of the two is their love of sailing the high seas. (*Author*)

And here are the lovely camera crew who undertook the filming and interviewing of Mr Walker outside his St Martin's Church Centre, August 2002. (*Author*)

St Martin's choirboys posing outside Shelley's chemist shop in Bank Street, *c.* 1953. Back row, left to right: crossbearer Roy Hollinshead, -?-. Centre row: Gordon Butler, -?-, -?-, Dennis Hickman, ? Walton. Front row: Barry Hill, Melvyn Rhodes, -?-, George Rogerson, Colin Edwards, John Hill, John Grinsell, Ray Jones. (*Derek Wood*)

A group from St Martin's gathering in Raleigh Road, Lower Bradley, during the 1950s. Here we see, from left to right: -?-, -?-, -?-, -?-, Mrs Lealan, Mary Davies, Mary Hatton. (*Derek Wood*)

The Chettles were a well-loved family in Bradley whose teacher daughters, Audrey and Rosamund, ran a special school at Innisfallen House, King Street. In this photograph those known are in the centre row only, from left to right: -?-, Mrs Lealan, Rosamund Chettle, -?-, Audrey Chettle, Mr Richard Buxton, Josie Bonical, Mrs Higgins and Mrs Gwen Thompson. (*Derek Wood*)

The St Martin's 1st Cub Group, *c.* 1975–6. They are in the St Francis Mission church, Willis Pearson Avenue, Lower Bradley. Back row, left to right: Leaders Chris Watson, Ann Wood and Sue Hazlehurst. Fourth row: -?-, -?-, Mark Wood, -?-, -?-, -?-, Michael Jackson, Neil Jones. Third row: Neil Stanford, ? Wildman, Paul Smith, Stephen Morgan, -?-, -?-, -?-, -?-, Jason Edwards. Second row: Dean Harriman, Steven Phillips, Philip Dicken, -?-, Wayne Bradley, Lee Anslow, Wayne Stanford, Darren Stanford. Front row: Simon Pugh, Julian Gold, ? Sneyd, David Haydn, Robert Joyce, David Smith, Andrew Hawksworth, Wayne Harriman. (*Derek Wood*)

The evening Carnival Dance was held in St Martin's School in 1967. The band had retired for refreshment and the local Scout lads took over the instruments. Here are, left to right, Carol Venton, John Grinsell, -?-, Graham Wilde, Derek Wood. (*Derek Wood*)

A Christmas fair at St Martin's Church, *c.* 1956. The name of the game is obscure, suffice to say it was a kind of skittles. Noted here are, left to right, Relief Vicar Davies, Derek Wood, Alan Richards, John Grinsell and Graham Pitt. (*Derek Wood*)

During the early 1930s, 1930–1 and 1932, respectively, as the photographs show, St Martin's school was blessed by having a teacher named Richard W. Earp, who besides being an author of local history also indulged himself as an amateur playwright of comic opera productions, which were very popular with the local community, especially at twopence for a programme and entrance. In the three photographs here and over the page, Earp is seen posing, either standing or sitting, centre, with the Revd C.O. Haden. The names of all who took part in the plays are noted in the programmes. (*Ray Barnsley*)

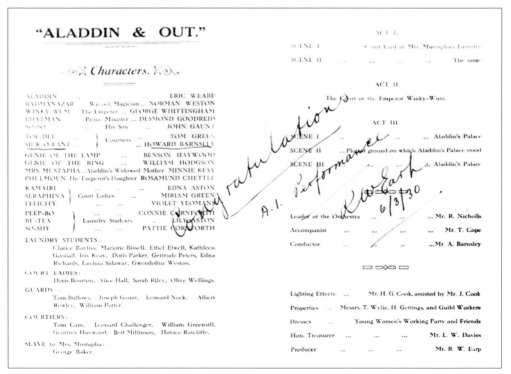

"ALADDIN & OUT."

Characters.

ALADDIN	...	ERIC WEARE
BADMANAZAR	Wicked Magician ...	NORMAN WESTON
WINKY-WUM	The Emperor ...	GEORGE WHITTINGHAM
PHATMAN	Prime Minister ...	DESMOND GOODREID
SO-SO	His Son ...	JOHN GAUNT
TOF-DEE	} Courtiers	TOM GREEN
SICK-O-FANT		HOWARD BARNSLEY
GENIE OF THE LAMP		BENSON HAYWOOD
GENIE OF THE RING	...	WILLIAM HODGSON
MRS. MUSTAPHA	Aladdin's Widowed Mother	MINNIE KEAY
PHULMOUN	The Emperor's Daughter	ROSAMUND CHETTLE
KAMAIRI	...	EDNA ASTON
SERAPHINA	} Court Ladies ...	MIRIAM GREEN
FELICITY	...	VIOLET YEOMANS
PEEP-BO	}	CONNIE CORNFORTH
BU-TEA	Laundry Students	LILY ASTON
SO-SHY	} ...	PATTIE CORNFORTH

LAUNDRY STUDENTS:
Clarice Bayliss, Marjorie Bissell, Ethel Elwell, Kathleen Goodall, Iris Keay, Doris Parker, Gertrude Peters, Edna Richards, Lavinia Sidaway, Gwendoline Weston.

COURT LADIES:
Doris Bourton, Alice Hall, Sarah Riley, Olive Wellings.

GUARDS:
Tom Bullows, Joseph Gaunt, Leonard Nock, Albert Rowley, William Potter.

COURTIERS:
Tom Cam, Leonard Challenger, William Greensill, Geoffrey Haywood, Bert Millinson, Horace Ratcliffe.

SLAVE to Mrs. Mustapha:
George Baker.

ACT I.
SCENE I   Court Yard at Mrs. Mustapha's Laundry
SCENE II   ...   .   The same

ACT II.
The Court of the Emperor Winky-Wum.

ACT III.
SCENE I   ...   . Aladdin's Palace
SCENE II   ... Ploughed ground on which Aladdin's Palace stood
SCENE III   ...   . Aladdin's Palace

Leader of the Orchestra	...	...	Mr. R. Nicholls
Accompanist	...	...	Mr. T. Cope
Conductor	...	...	Mr. A. Barnsley

Lighting Effects	...	Mr. H. G. Cook, assisted by Mr. J. Cook
Properties	...	Messrs. T. Wylie, H. Gettings, and Guild Workers
Dresses	...	Young Women's Working Party and Friends
Hon. Treasurer	...	...	Mr. L. W. Davies
Producer	...	...	Mr. R. W. Earp

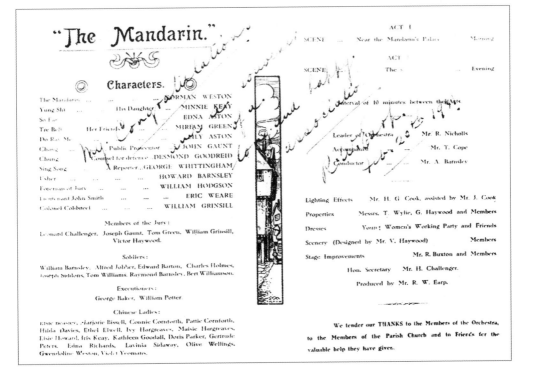

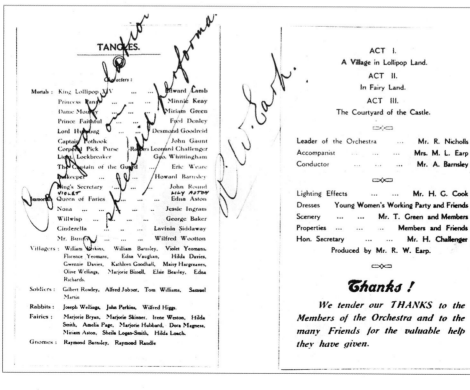

TANGLES.

Characters:

Mortals:
King Lollipop XIV	... ...	Edward Lamb
Princess Fancy	... ...	Minnie Keay
Dame Mousey	... ...	Miriam Green
Prince Faithful	... ...	Fred Denley
Lord Humbug	... ...	Desmond Goodreid
Captain Pothook	...	John Gaunt
Corporal Pick Purse	...Leonard Challenger
Lieut. Lockbreaker	...	Geo. Whittingham
The Captain of the Guard	...	Eric Weare
Lockkeeper	...	Howard Barnsley
King's Secretary	...	John Round

Immortals:
Queen of Fairies	... ...	Edna Aston
Nona	... ...	Jessie Ingram
Willwisp	... ...	George Baker
Cinderella	... ...	Lavinia Siddaway
Mr. Bunny	... ...	Wilfred Wootton

Villagers: William Perkins, William Barnsley, Violet Yeomans, Florence Yeomans, Edna Vaughan, Hilda Davies, Gwennie Davies, Kathleen Goodhall, Maisy Hargreaves, Olive Wellings, Marjorie Bissell, Elsie Beasley, Edna Richards.

Soldiers: Gilbert Rowley, Alfred Jobber, Tom Williams, Samuel Martin

Rabbits: Joseph Wellings, John Perkins, Wilfred Higgs.

Fairies: Marjorie Bryan, Marjorie Skinner, Irene Weston, Hilda Smith, Amelia Page, Marjorie Hubbard, Dora Magness, Miriam Aston, Sheila Logan-Smith, Hilda Loach.

Gnomes: Raymond Barnsley, Raymond Randle

ACT I.
A Village in Lollipop Land.

ACT II.
In Fairy Land.

ACT III.
The Courtyard of the Castle.

◇✕◇

Leader of the Orchestra	...	Mr. R. Nicholls
Accompanist	... ...	Mrs. M. L. Earp
Conductor	... ...	Mr. A. Barnsley

◇✕◇

Lighting Effects	... ...	Mr. H. G. Cook
Dresses	Young Women's Working Party and Friends
Scenery	... ...	Mr. T. Green and Members
Properties	...	Members and Friends
Hon. Secretary	... ...	Mr. H. Challenger

Produced by Mr. R. W. Earp.

◇✕◇

Thanks !

We tender our THANKS to the Members of the Orchestra and to the many Friends for the valuable help they have given.

Pupils of Class 10 in St Martin's School, *c*. 1935. Those present are, at the back, Mr Haywood, headmaster, Miss Gilbey. Back row, standing, left to right, -?-, -?-, -?-, ? Hazlehurst, -?-, -?-, -?-, Dennis Gilbey. Fourth row: -?-, Phyllis Davies, -?-, Jean Hawks, -?-, -?-. Third row: Ray Barnsley, Doris Loach, Irene Rowley, Violet Windmill, -?-, -?-. Second row: Connie Webb, -?-, Norma Mitton, Bert Haywood, Mary Peters, Joan Walton. Front row: -?-, Ray Parker, -?-, -?-. Standing down the side: -?-, -?-, Ina Bryan, -?-, -?-, Ruby Hargreaves. (*Ray Barnsley*)

Another class at St Martin's School, 1952. This is Miss Jackson's sewing class, and seen from left to right are, Maureen ?, Marie ?, Pauline Lucas, Christine Burgess, Pauline Peeler and Norma Hammond. (*Norma Hammond*)

This climbing frame seems to have been a popular feature at St Martin's. The children enjoying the facility in 1952 are, from the back, Roy Ellis, John Norman and John Bowker, then Wendy Higginson, Carol Williams, (the late) Beryl Rowley, (the late) Elaine Lloyd and Beryl Brown. At the front, Joan Rickuss. (*Joan Rickuss*)

Still with St Martin's School, this is Mr Boydon's class, 1953. Back row, left to right: ? Ingram, Patrick Hickinbottom. Sixth row: Peter Fieldhouse, -?-, -?-. Fifth row: Michael Granger and Derek Higginson. Fourth row: ? Russon, -?-, -?-. Third row: (the late) Ruth Nailor, Lilian Picken. Second row: Joan Rickuss, Elaine Lloyd. Front, Carol Williams. (*Joan Rickuss*)

An old, all boys, St Martin's School group photograph, 1916. Most are wearing the large white starched collars of the time, but the names and faces have long passed into obscurity, except two; these are David Rickuss, in the third row, third from the left, and John Grinsell, second row, sixth from the left. (*Joan Rickuss*)

The late Mr and Mrs D. Rickuss are seen here during a holiday in Paignton in 1976. Mrs Rickuss, along with Mrs Webb and Mrs Picken, served dinners at St Martin's School for many years and will no doubt be fondly remembered by many readers. (*Joan Rickuss*)

This smart young fellow with polished boots and cane in hand is David Rickuss Sr, seen in 1915. David became a Regimental Sergeant Major in the Staffordshire Regiment. (*Joan Rickuss*)

This mid-1960s photograph shows the Crown and Cushion public house in the final days of its existence, and even though a newer Crown and Cushion was built on the opposite diagonal corner, it somehow proved to be the end of an era. (*Ron Davies Collection*)

A society wedding in Bradley? It would appear so; the year was 1914 and the wedding that of Norris and Kitty Eccleston. The photograph was taken in the grounds of Devon House in King Street. None can be identified in the back row. Second row, left to right: Harry Eccleston Sr, -?-, -?-, -?-, -?-, Norris and Kitty Eccleston, Grandad Eccleston, Great-Gran Eccleston, George Eccleston, Walter Eccleston, -?-. Front row: -?-, -?-, -?-, -?-, Gran Eccleston, -?-. Sitting on the ground: -?-, Percy Eccleston, -?-, -?-. (*Beth Aston*)

A happy group of Bradley urchins, *c.* 1930. Faces and names are difficult to place but the blond-headed lad on the back row, just off centre, is Bert Williams, who became the noted Wolves goal-keeper of the 1940s and '50s. (*Roy Hawthorne Collection*)

A weekend trip from the Crown and Cushion to Morecambe, organised by Mrs Gladys Broadley, sees the group posing for a little get-together outside their holiday digs. (*Ron Perry*)

A Sunday morning breakfast trip to Ironbridge from the Crown and Cushion, 1949. Back row, left to right: -?-, Stan Whitehouse, Bill Yeoman, Dick Yeoman, Arthur Caddick, Mr Caddick Sr. Third row: Mr Loach, Bill Nash, Dick Yeoman Sr, -?-. Second row wearing a mortar-board, Cala Vaughan. Front row, sitting and squatting: Bill Burgess, Mr Burgess Sr, Harold Books, Ron Perry, Mr Cole. Sitting on the bench by the river is Mr Bennett. (*Ron Perry*)

Yet another Sunday morning outing from the Crown and Cushion, *c.* 1950. Those in the picture, from left to right, are Jim Horton, Ron Perry, Joe Downes, Horace Britten, Jack Richards, Horace Skinner. The location of this trip is unknown, other than being somewhere in the countryside. (*Ron Perry*)

Life was never dull at the Crown and Cushion. Here landlady Elsie Yeoman poses with some of her bar helpers, *c.* 1962. From left to right we see Marie Morgan, Mary Richards, Bill Yeoman, Elsie Yeoman, Albert Morgan and Eileen Gillard. (*Harold Humphries*)

Another bar shot; here Mrs Yeoman enjoys a moment with Mary Richards and her son Bill, *c.* 1962. In the background can be seen Horace Ratcliffe. (*Harold Humphries*)

Though slightly double exposed, this shot is nevertheless a rare view of Bank Street in about 1966. Nearest to the camera is Harold and Dorrie Smallman's general and off-licence store; beyond it is a lovely row of old cottages, the end one of which was Downing's bicycle and accessories shop. (*Ron Davies Collection*)

These are the children (and a few parents) of Walter Road estate celebrating the Queen's Coronation in 1953. Among them are Margaret Flavell, Ken Flavell, Linda Flavell, Pauline Flavell, Tony Bateman, Beryl Durnal, Fred Durnal, Ray Clarke, Teddy Amos, Wilfred Amos, Derek Wood, John Stokes, John Cox, Mr Wildman and daughter, Patrick Sullivan, Betty Wildman, Tony Stokes, Elva Wysdale, Margaret Watson, George Proud, Sylvia Forshaw, Gwen Forshaw, Billy Butler, Jimmy Butler, Brian Butler, Ray Butler, Mary Stokes, Barbara Webb, Roy Challoner, Derek Watson, Brian Watson, Barbara Ratcliffe and Jean Greaves. (*Margaret Flavell*)

Brenda Beech (née Morris) of Victoria, British Columbia, Canada, comes up with some more nostalgic photographs. This one was taken in about 1925, by her Grandad Tunnicliffe at 7 Martin Road. She said he pulled a black cloth over his head while taking photographs, which always scared her. She is seen here with her Aunt Bertha; behind are cousins Alan and Peggy Laycock, of Woodhouse, Yorkshire. Peggy (later Young) moved to Bishopbriggs, Glasgow, where she started the Women's Voluntary Service. She died in the mid-1980s. (*Brenda Beech*)

This *c.* 1929 Martin Road picture, though now rather faded, shows from left to right, Peggy Boucher/Holland, now of Southampton, May Boucher/Jordan, of Tettenhall and Brenda Morris/Beech, Canada. These girls are still in touch with each other after all these years. (*Brenda Beech*)

Here is Brenda Beech on one of her rare visits home, posing with her cousin Enid Tunnicliffe (right) in Hannah Road, Lower Bradley, July 1950. (*Brenda Beech*)

One of the sights to be seen in Walter Road during the 1940s–50s was Mr Lealan's Austin Lichfield motor car. It last saw duty in 1953, when after a busy coronation day it met with an accident which caused it to be written off. As you see by the state of the car, there was no such thing as an MOT in those days to ensure one could travel safely. (*Derek Wood*)

This shot was taken from the site of the former Matthews' foundry. In the background are St Martin's Church, the Wilkinson school and the remains of John Wilkinson's slag heap. The embankment to the left is where the old Upper Bradley blast furnace stood. An archaeological dig on the site in 1960 revealed industrial foundations, and certain iron artefacts were deposited in Bilston Museum. (*Author*)

A trio of Wilkinson Avenue youngsters pose by the Memorial Cross in the Coronation Park, which at that time, 1938, was securely fenced off. On the left is Geoffrey Smith, with Doreen Beards and her brother Ron. (*Doreen Pye*)

A quiet sit-down at the side of Bradley Pool that was, *c.* 1955. The young man on the left is unknown; on the right is Geoffrey Smith. The background shows the Niagara foundry with its simple cupola stack. (*Eric Pugh*)

This drawing shows John Wilkinson's furnace in Hall Fields, now Wilkinson Avenue. Wednesbury church can be clearly seen in the background. Also visible are Wilkinson's middle works followed by the cones of the Bradley Pottery, then the Fiery Holes furnace (in between the middle works and the pottery). Seen in the distance are Moorcroft furnaces. All the industry is long forgotten, for the area is now residential. The original of this scene, a watercolour of 1835 by Robert Noyes, is in the Salt Library, Stafford. (*Author*)

These iron artefacts, formerly housed in Bilston Museum, are those discovered during an archaeological dig on the Hall Fields furnace site in 1960. Such cast-iron pipes as seen here were typical of Wilkinson's noted products, and were generally still being made to carry water, sewage, etc. until the advent of plastic. (*Author*)

Further artefacts gleaned from the Wilkinson
furnace site. These appear to be test pieces and
some sections of angle iron. (*Author*)

This grandfather clock is another feature believed to
have come down from the Wilkinson era. There was
also a fireplace, and both were donated to Bilston
Museum in about 1938 by Mrs Edwards of Bradley,
whose forebears were servants in the Wilkinson
household. She also was said to have had his legs!
No doubt these were wooden ones, used to keep his
breeches on, to keep them in good shape. (*Author*)

Though somewhat faded now, this little family scene from 1924 was taken outside 6 Adams Row, Cross Street. Here we see, from left to right, Bett Stevens (now Gripton) with brothers Jack, sitting on the chair, and George. Jack died at the early age of four from diptheria, which at that time was an endemic infection. (*George Stevens*)

Another picture in the same yard and under the same window shows Bett Stevens, now growing up, with little sister Irene sitting on her dad's knee, *c.* 1926. Their father was George Stevens Sr. (*George Stevens*)

During one of his rare visits to call on his brother Dr Charles Slim at Bradley, Lieutenant-General (later Viscount Field-Marshal) Sir William Slim of the 'forgotten' 14th Army in Burma, was inevitably called on as a special celebrity to talk to the dignitaries at Bilston Town Hall, where he was given a civic welcome. Also present in the picture are the Drs Slim, Charles and his wife Kathleen, though they are almost hidden behind the plant on the table. The date was Saturday 23 June 1945. The war in Europe was over, the Japanese in Burma were on the run and Japan was soon to be the victim of an atom bomb at Hiroshima on 6 August 1945. (*Donated by Ray Barnsley. Express and Star*)

It is nice that some Christmas cards come down through the ages; this rare one could be from either the 1930s or '40s, but is probably wartime owing to its simplicity. It was sent by Drs Charles and Kathleen Slim. (*Ray Barnsley*)

As with the Crown and Cushion in Bank Street, so the Golden Lion (Smithy's) in Ash Street also kept its customers happy with Sunday morning trips. Here standing in front of a Don Everall coach are, from left to right, Floss Humphries, Violet Homfray and Alice Lane, *c.* 1949. (*Harold Humphries*)

This is a group photograph on the same occasion. To name a few, not in order: ? Summers, Alice Lane, H. Humphries, Violet Rock, Noreen Evans and Mrs Southall. Violet Homfray is second from left; far right is Floss Humphries. (*Violet Rock*)

Another 1950s Sunday morning trip from the Golden Lion, only it's the men this time. Charlie Morgan, Joe Richards and Ben Rock are among those present. (*Harold Humphries*)

The same Sunday morning trip, and at the back are Ben Rock (left) and H. Humphries. In front, Bill Rock and Dan Rock. (*Harold Humphries*)

There's no doubt about it, Bradley folk loved a day trip and the staff of Barnsley's Brass Foundry in Lane Street were no exception. There are lots of remembered faces here, all posing outside boss Mr William Barnsley's house in Lane Street in 1948. Back row, left to right: Freddie Hackett, Jackie Pountney, Howard Barnsley, Colin Barnsley, J. Ashfield, Albert Cooper and Alan Withers. Third row: Frank Kidson, Ben Bissell, Jonto Ray, Vic Hawkins, Joe Moore, Howard Freeman, Finney Gough, Kenny Gough, Charlie Millard, Jimmy Wooldridge, Roy Richards, Harry Rickuss, Jack Dale and Gordon Gough. Second row: Marjorie Potts, Dolly Pritchard, Maisie Hargreaves, Audrey Sandland, Joan Taylor, Ellen Salt and Rose Barnes. Front row: Betty Hackett, Violet Waller, Emmie Hadley, Mrs Magness, Ellie Fellows, Nancy Pritchard, Connie Hibbs, Beattie Harris, Emmie Lloyd and Beattie Griffiths. Lying comfortably or uncomfortably in front is the boss, William Barnsley; in a much more comfortable position is Alf Barnsley; the man wearing a trilby hat is Walter Pritchard; and next, wearing a cap, is Joe Fellows. The occasion is a works outing to Matlock Bath, Derbyshire. (*Ray Barnsley*)

Barnsley's employees on a day trip and lunch to Windsor, 1950s. (*Ray Barnsley*)

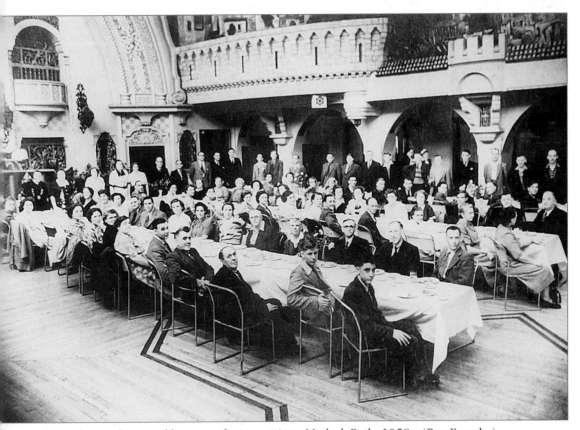

Barnsley's employees share a table or two during a trip to Matlock Bath, 1950s. (*Ray Barnsley*)

This particular commemorative carving, now deteriorating badly, lies on the site of the former railway track, near the old bridge between Ash Street and Daisy Street. Whether this particular engine, the 'Iron Duke', ever passed through here is debatable, but it's a nice thought. As can be seen, engine drivers then were a hardy breed, with no cab to protect them from the elements. (*Author*)

A doorstep scene at 2 Ash Street, 1948. These are three daughters of the Eccleston family, from left to right, Miriam, Betty, Pat and Rover the dog. (*Betty Aston*)

In the early 1950s the Second World War was still fresh in people's minds, as demonstrated in this Wesleyan parade in Hall Green Street. The children were known as Lifeboys. The centre leader is Beryl Phillips and on the extreme left is Vi Fletcher, now Grainger. The background is where Dr Lal now has his surgery, and the building on the left was the local post office, run by Mr Whitehouse. This is still standing at present, through the building with the stone or ashlar façade has gone. Behind the wall stood the Primitive Methodist chapel, and the far building was a general provisions shop run by Mrs Griffiths. (*Roy Hawthorne Collection*)

This is the same scene today. The building on the left is the old post office, now cladded with a stone mixture. Its future is uncertain. The far building is the Great Western public house. (*Author*)

This wide-angle view was taken from the old post office soon after all the old houses in John, Chell and Stoke Streets had been demolished, leaving only the Golden Lion public house, seen to the left as a white gabled building, and Paddock's the cobblers about centre. Slim Avenue is in the right background and Ash Street with its old houses and school is on the left; the road going down the middle was John Street, which still exists in part. (*Ken Fellows*)

Another wide-angle shot shows what the above scene looks like today. It shows what little is left of John Street, and the rest is dominated by council flats and garages. (*Author*)

Views of the Stoke Street area are rare indeed, and thanks to the following carnival scenes one can get an idea of how this area once looked. One thing is certain, Bradley folk of old loved a carnival! This crowded scene in Stoke Street marks the start of the Coronation Carnival in 1953. (*Ken Fellows*)

Another Stoke Street carnival scene. The lean-to building with the two chimneys, where generally the weekly wash was carried out, was typically referred to as a 'brewce' or brew house. (*Ken Fellows*)

Here are two special shots of the Carnival Queen and her attendants taken in Stoke Street. The question is, who were they?

To show the effort that went into these carnivals, here are three lads dressed as gentlemen of the road and doing it remarkably well. They are from left to right, Lennie Bradbury, Bertie Martin and Dennis Turner. (*Ken Fellows*)

The gentlemen of the road are seen posing with other carnival participants. A few names here are, back row, tall girl with medal, Pauline Fellows. Front row, left to right: Dennis Turner, Bertie Martin, Maureen Lockley, -?-, Pat Maydew, the little nurse, Susan Hatton, Roma Fellows, -?-, Lennie Bradbury. (*Ken Fellows*)

Another aspect of the Coronation Carnival was called Sporting Personalities. Left to right are cricketers Len Hutton and Fred Truman; the boxer is Randolph Turpin, the footballer Billy Wright, and posing as jockey Lester Piggott is Roy Squires. (*Ken Fellows*)

Lady Sporting Personalities include, from right to left, tennis champions Gussie and Little Mo, swimmer Diane Wilkinson, world skating champion Jeanette Altwegg, the Blue Flash and Angela Barwell. (*Ken Fellows*)

A bevy of beauties, a spring scene perhaps, from the 1951 carnival. (*Ken Rellows*)

More beauty as these girls seem to be acting out their fantasies, 1951. They would all be around their early fifties now and are probably still around. The number of the door in Stoke Street is 22. (*Ken Fellows*)

The procession carries on with this Robin Hood caper, 1951. (*Ken Fellows*)

The procession has now moved on into Hall Green Street and is approaching Ash Street, this time with an Old Mother Riley character, 1951. (*Ken Fellows*)

After a busy carnival parade, sports were held on Udall's field in Daisy Street. This race sees the girls in full flight. (*Ken Fellows*)

Still on Udall's field, it is now the boys' turn to show their running ability. (*Ken Fellows*)

After the parade, after the sports, it becomes time for a party such as this to be held at the Wesleyan chapel. (*Ken Fellows*)

Some of the weary parents at the Coronation party held at the Wesleyan chapel. The picture includes Joe Hall, Jack Morgan, Clem Pierce, Mr Bailey, Harold and Floss Humphries, Derek Dudley, Mrs Slater, Edith Smith and Dot Maydew. (*Ken Fellows*)

In 1998 the Patients Voice Group of the Bradley Medical Centre gather at Wombourne ready
for a sponsored walk along its former railway track, mainly in aid of the Marie Curie Fund and
the Bradley Medical Centre. Back row, left to right: Roy Loach, Jean Sneyd, Ray Tuft. Middle
row: John Guest, Doreen Loach, Susan Differ, Sharda Verma, Irene Tuft. Front row: Karen
Sutton, Claire Sutton, Terry Sneyd. (*Bradley Medical Centre*)

The Patients Voice Group are seen at the Medical Centre to present an ECG machine to Dr Lal for
his practice, donated from their funds. Back row, left to right: Ray Tuft, Jean Sneyd. Middle row:
Irene Tuft, Karen Sutton, Jackie Brettle. Front row: John Guest, Josie Brown, Olwen Warwick,
Eileen Wright. Seen presenting the machine to Dr Lal is Arthur Wright. (*Bradley Medical Centre*)

The latest sponsored walk along the Wombourne Railway Walk, organised by the Hall Green Street Medical Centre Patients Voice Group, in aid of the Macmillan Nurses and the Medical Centre, took place on 11 May 2002. The day started chilly but towards noon it really became hot. This drawing shows Terry Sneyd, long a helper at the medical centre, taking a well-earned breather close to the finishing point. (*Author*)

Before the First World War the Shoulder of Mutton (the Fourpenny Shop) public house in Hall Green Street was run by Mr Albert Davies. Here is his family: his wife Sarah with, from left to right, Richard, Liza, Violet and Albert. Violet, now aged ninety-two, is the only remaining member of the group. (*Beryl Pugh*)

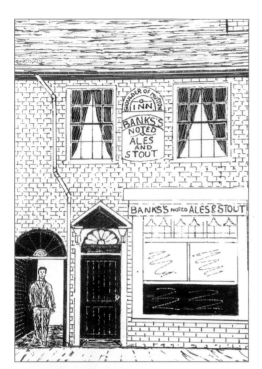

This sketch shows the front of the Shoulder of Mutton in Hall Green Street, *c.* 1960. (*Author*)

A rare view of Hall Green Street, *c.* 1965. The children are playing outside an off-licence, and the houses on the right of the picture are, from right to left, Bennion's house, Cox's general provisions, Callaway's greengrocery, -?-, the Shoulder of Mutton, Higgins Bakery, Kate Hammond's sweet shop and at the end Bert Garvey, Printers. In the distance is Wootton's house and then the Britannia public house. (*Ken Fellows*)

A lot of smiling faces on this Wesleyan trip to Trentham Gardens, *c.* 1950. Here grouped on the steps are a few well-known chapel members: Mr Sam Bailey, Mr and Mrs J. Grinsell, Mr and Mrs A. Beddows, Miss Taylor, Mrs Phillips, Miss Fletcher, Miss Edna Boyd, Mr Coulson, Carol Round, Benita Hammond, Mavis Jones, Bernard Davies, Dorothy Reynolds, Elsie Reynolds, ? Hinks, June Hird, Maggie George, Iris George, Geoffrey George, Mrs Reynolds, Wilfy Mullard and Dorothy Jones. (*Roy Hawthorne*)

A Wesleyan anniversary scene behind the chapel. Noted here, back row, left, Eva Bailey, back row, right, Evelyn Smith, and Arthur Beddows at centre left. One of the children is Norma Hammond; another is Margaret Armstrong, centre right with the long darkish hair. (*Harold Humphries. Roy Hawthorne*)

Arthur Gough leads the Wesleyan Boys' Brigade at Abergele, on the occasion of the brigade's first outing after the Second World War, 1946. Jack Newell is seen in the front row far right. (*Roy Hawthorne*)

This happy scene shows Margaret and Alan Wootton enjoying a bit of summer sunshine at 18 Chapel Yard, Hall Green Street, in 1953. (*Arthur Wootton*)

Emily Kinsey of Hall Green Street poses with her bicycle, *c.* 1950. (*Emily Kinsey*)

Emily Kinsey poses on the Hilly with a friend, *c.* 1950. (*Emily Kinsey*)

Seen on the Hilly are, from left to right, Anna Mills, -?-, and Emily Kinsey, *c.* 1950. Note St Aidan's Mission in the background. (*Emily Kinsey*)

Still on the Hilly, two boys stop their game of football to pose for the camera in the mid-1970s; note the old type of leather case-ball. St Aidan's Mission is missing; instead, the Wesleyan chapel dominates the background. (*Ken Fellows*)

This jolly lady is Mrs Jones, *c.* 1952. She kept a little grocery shop in Hall Green Street. As was possible in those days, she turned the front room of her house into a shop, so the window you see was the shop window. Lots of people turned spare rooms into shops to augment their low incomes, especially during the 1930s and '40s, but the Slum Clearance Act put an end to this type of living. (*Emily Kinsey*)

Just one more Coronation Carnival scene. Taken in Hall Green Street those present are, from left to right, -?-, two Reynolds girls in pinafores and carnival hats, Harriet Mills and Emily Jones. Sitting is old Bradley character Jody Whacker. (*Polly Shepherd*)

A splendid view of the Britannia Inn, Hall Green Street, during the 1960s. The couple outside are landlords Frank and Violet Poole. (*Reg Aston*)

A proud moment in the Britannia when the darts champions show off their trophies, possibly in the 1970s. Named are B. Nicholls and B. Walton. (*Author's Collection*)

Shopkeepers Irene and Olive Roberts stand outside their shop in Hall Green Street. There is little to be seen in the way of advertising other than the Heinz 57 symbols. The house and the shop were the last of the old buildings to be demolished in the street, and the picture is from *c.* 1980. (*Ray Barnsley*)

The whole of the Roberts' property before it was demolished. It was quite a sound and substantial building. Its site still lies fallow, but the two pubs, the George & Dragon and the Britannia on the right, are still with us. (*Ray Barnsley*)

Ben Smith was a popular coach proprietor in Bradley. Here in the 1930s he poses with his family and driver on what appears to be the end of Blackpool Pier. From left to right are Mrs Hallmark of Cross Street, Ben Smith, driver George Butler, Mrs Smith and son Bert, and sitting are nephews Wilf Hallmark (left) and his brother Stan. (*Arthur Wootton*)

This fine young man standing in Wesley Street in 1914 is William Thomas Morris. Tommy was then serving in the South Staffordshire Regiment. (*Brenda Beech*)

What happened to Tommy Morris in the First World War is uncertain, but one lad from Wesley Street never came back from the Second World War, as this headstone shows. This was Ronnie Norman of the Black Watch, who was killed on 27 September 1944. He was a very talented pianist and could have gone far in the musical world. Alas, there is no known photograph of him. (*Myra Thompson*)

This is a general view of the Military Cemetery at St Omer, where Ronnie Norman and many others now rest. The photograph taken by Ronnie's sister Myra Thompson shows the dedication that goes into the care of these cemeteries, which we hope will provide some comfort to others who lost loved ones on the battlefields of France. (*Myra Thompson*)

This view, looking south from the Hilly, shows where the old railway line ran before being axed. The bridge over which ran the traffic along Brierley Lane has been levelled and the whole site is now a cemetery. The former Bricklayers Arms pub is seen on the right and the Vogue Bath foundry cupola is seen directly ahead, *c.* 1980. (*Author*)

Looking south-east from the Hilly, *c.* 1960, the newly established Batmans Hill estate can be seen. On the extreme left of the scene is one of the last old houses in Brierley Lane. (*Ken Fellows*)

This happy scene was captured in Batmans Hill Road in the early 1930s. The lads looking very smart in their blue serge suits and school caps are, from left to right, Harold, Bill and Arthur Wootton; the lovely lass dressed in white is their cousin Mary Smith. (*Arthur Wootton*)

The Vogue Bath cupola was a local landmark. This is a view looking down Flavell Avenue just over the border in Coseley; it dominated this area for quite a number of years. (*Author*)

These are the Vogue foundry staff awaiting the arrival of the last bath to come into view. They know their jobs are at an end, and this is an awful but nostalgic moment for them. (*Arthur Wootton*)

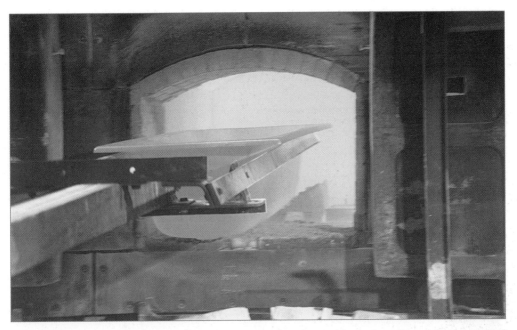

In their day Vogue baths were of the highest quality, but with the coming of fibreglass and plastic all the skills that went into the production of cast-iron baths were lost. This shows the last bath going through the final stages of production, being drawn out of the annealing furnace red-hot, ready to have the enamel powder sprayed over it to give it its finishing touch. (*Arthur Wootton*)

Here the last bath comes into view. I wonder whose home it eventually graced. (*Arthur Wootton*)

From one foundry to another in the late 1950s. These are the pattern-makers busy at Matthews' spick and span foundry in Cross Street. Here, from left to right, are Len Kinsey, Lew Mole (on the lathe), Ken Cooper, Les ?, Arthur Summerfield and Jack Beards. (*Edward Matthews Ltd*)

These are girls from the accounts and wages department of Edward Matthews, enjoying a dance at Bilston Town Hall, *c.* 1955. From left to right are Beryl Partridge (née Page), Doreen Challenor and Iris Clarke (née Griffiths). (*Iris Griffiths*)

A few more of Matthews' office staff, *c.* 1957, this time enjoying a summer lunch break on the handy and lovely open space of the Rocket, so called owing to the plant rocket that once flourished here and a land area formerly known as Rocket Piece. The general background shows the Thompson Brothers works, with Wednesbury church in the far distance and the Rocket pools at the top right. This was once a delightful wildlife area, but an ever-increasing population and slum clearance meant that houses came first. The pool, however, still remains. The girls are, left to right: Iris Griffiths, Dorothy Fullwood, Joyce Lowe and Iris Bull. (*Iris Griffiths*)

Still with Edward Matthews staff but now on the far side of the Rocket pools, and actually on the side of Bradley Locks. Note the ancient tippings created by the Wednesbury Oak furnaces, whose works ceased production soon after the First World War. Seen here are, from left to right, Iris Griffiths, Dot Fullwood, Iris Bull, -?- and Joyce Lowe, *c.* 1957. (*Iris Griffiths*)

British Waterways Department in Bradley Lane has a fine record when it comes to making lock gates. Here, sketched in about 1995, we have one coming to completion, being worked on by Mark Ashlee and apprentice Carl Harris (left). Other work is also carried out here: making signposts, gates, benches, fencing, etc., all of the finest quality. (*Author*)

One celebrity canal enthusiast to visit the Bradley Waterways workshop is David Suchet of Poirot fame, who made a special journey along this old Brindley cul-de-sac during the last week of January 2002. David is the Vice-President of the Lichfield and Hatherton Canals Restoration Trust. (*Gavin Dickson, Express and Star*)

3

Ladymoor

As slag heaps go, this one, laid down over a period of at least 100 years from the Capponfield furnaces, was by far the largest in the area. This north end of the heap, as seen from Coseley Road during the 1930s and '40s, was in a molten glassy state, so for us kids it was quite impossible to negotiate, but a cleft further along allowed one to climb to the top, where grew masses of wall pepper (a moss-like plant with yellow star-like flowers). It was also frequented by rabbits. The railway fence, like all local railway fences, was made of birch, which lasted for years. (*Author*)

The south end of the slag heap was craggy but paths were easy and allowed one closer contact with this man-made mountain. Slag heaps were said to be eyesores but wildlife such as one never or rarely sees today flourished here in all its forms. The demise of the slag heaps came about for several reasons: to be crushed to create roads, to build walls and buildings, and to fashion what we call breeze blocks for house building. Certain parts known as tap cinder were especially sought out as they were iron-rich and used to feed back into the furnace. Coalbrookdale uses the hard glassy greenish slags to fashion jewellery. The furnace waste was never wasted. (*Harry Eccleston*)

A train pulls out of Coseley Road station bound for Dudley and Worcester, Evesham or Hereford. Racing pigeons were transported regularly, and workers to and from all quarters; at harvest time, for example, hop pickers were ferried into Herefordshire. Iron ore came from Northampton to feed the furnaces; and wholesalers Wallett and Rowley relied heavily on the rail service for their supplies of fruit and vegetables. Note the last remains of the slag heap, in front of which can be seen the neatly stacked building blocks formed out of the limestone slag. Some of these still remain on the site. The road bending off to the right once led into Capponfield. (*Harry Eccleston*)

Scrap heaps were never the most picturesque of scenes, but if Harry Eccleston had not recorded them, such industrial activities would have been lost for local posterity. This is a simple gantry through which, in the background, one can faintly make out the complex of the Spring Vale steelworks. The scrap was intended for the Capponfield cupola of Bradley and Foster, who specialised in the manufacture of shot (small round grain sized bits of iron) that could be blasted through a nozzle, mainly to clean iron castings; the photograph dates from the mid-1960s. (*Harry Eccleston*)

This gantry scene is one of a series of etchings crafted by Harry Eccleston of the Capponfield gantry, which he named 'The Capponfield Suite'. This is no. 7 of the collection. (*Harry Eccleston*)

This sketch, after a watercolour by William Kape, a former principal of Bilston Art School, is looking from Capponfield towards Spring Vale works and the houses that once lined this quarter of Broad Lanes. The names of some former residents are still remembered from the '30s: the Bankses, the Bunces, the Hawkins, the Lathams, the Gearys, the Evanses, the Phillips, the Bristows, the Pottses, the Paynes, the Wrights, the Morrises, the Davies and the Carons, who lived in the former army hut residence. (*Author*)

The George & Dragon, better known as the Clog, is the only remaining pub in the area. Its situation has been uncertain in recent years, as this scene shows, but it has once again been given a reprieve and is now under new management. (*Author*)

Every Sunday morning Harry Eccleston visited his Uncle Bill and Aunt Eliza Latham at their cottage in Moor Street, mainly to execute this drawing of them in their parlour. Harry said, 'It must have been done in the summer because I had to sit on the hob to do it'. It is typical of the time, 1949, showing the ubiquitous table (probably scrubbed top and covered only on Sundays) and sideboard with mirror and chiming clock, no airs and graces here. Bill worked at the steelworks as did virtually all the Latham family. This particular cottage belonged to the works. Bill's father, John Henry, after an accident, worked in the stables; one of his tasks was to drive the ambulance, the one mentioned and shown earlier (see p. 42) (*Harry Eccleston*)

Until about 1940 Tenscore footbridge was a noted thoroughfare to and from Bilston town. It was used by steelworkers and residents who lived in the scattered cottages to the west of the bridge. Local boys also came to swim in the warm canal waters, provided with heat by the adjacent steelworks. (*Andrew Barnett*)

Looking west from Tenscore bridge during the 1930s, the scars and heaps from the Spring Vale colliery and other small pits were beginning to heal over. Trees were planted on the colliery site in about 1906 to become known as Tenscore Forest; many rare plants flourished here, but blackberries were most loved and basketfuls were harvested. The house seen on the left by the pool was where the Richards family lived, and the cottage by the side of the path found the Broadhursts. The whole area became a Site of Special Scientific Interest Grade 1, but the need for more land on which to tip the furnace waste in the 1970s overruled this. Today it is covered by the Sedgemoor housing estate. (*Author*)

This rare scene, from the 1926 coal strike, was painted by Andrew Barnett, and is set on the former Tenscore coalfields. It shows ordinary folk mining for coal to keep the home fires burning. As there was no electricity then and very little gas, most folk relied on coal for cooking and warmth, and oil or candles for light. Fortunately the shallow coals lay close to the surface here, and any surplus coals dug were usually sold off to the middlemen. The strikes, however, proved disastrous and virtually ended all coal mining in the area, because the mines became flooded. (*Andrew Barnett*)

Another 1926 scene captured by Andrew Barnett, this time in Ladymoor. Cottages such as this were once a common feature in the area. The Lilley family lived here at that time and seemed to have an idyllic way of life with a wonderful sense of freedom, although beyond the cot lay the LMS (London, Midland & Scottish), or Stour Valley railway line. (*Andrew Barnett*)

Where once the Lilleys' cottage stood became the victim of furnace tippings and scrap heaps. Boys, however, always seemed to find somewhere to have a game of football. Note the different paths that the workers had made journeying to and from their labours in the works beyond. This photograph dates from the early 1960s. (*Harry Eccleston*)

More or less on the same spot as above, this scrap scene was meticulously portrayed by Harry Eccleston, who loved and recorded the industrial scene whenever possible, even though at times it meant travelling from his London home to do so. I suppose this scene could be called 'Knocking Off', as it shows workmen passing by the scrap on their way home at the end of their Spring Vale shift, 1960. (*Harry Eccleston*)

A general view of Ladymoor as it was in 1947. The Brickmakers Arms was the first building on the left, and the houses on the right still remain. Otherwise nothing is left, other than the trees near the centre of the picture, which mark the site of the former chapel. (*Author*)

Wedding photographs are an unusual feature in these pages, but this particular wedding was the first to be held in the Ladymoor chapel, simply because there had been nowhere to keep the documents concerned with such events. The groom was Bill Grinsell, and his bride was Jean Dugmore, who was the organist here. It was her father, local coal merchant William Dugmore, who provided a safe in which to keep marriage records and other important chapel items. The marriage was conducted on 29 August 1953. (*Bill Grinsell*)

Over the years, Ladymoor chapel had a faithful congregation and when some members were killed in action during the First World War, memorial plaques were thought best to honour their heroes. Since the demolition of the chapel, the plaques have been in the safe keeping of Sedgley Museum in Brick Street. (*Author*)

Here, young Geoffrey Barnsley poses with his faithful hound at his bungalow home, *c.* 1955. The background shows part of old Ladymoor. The Davies lived in the house on the left which was next door to the Brickmakers Arms. The house had long been the home of the Humpage family, next came the Dykes and on the other side of the entry was Jones's shop. The enamel sign over the entry states simply 'Hudson's Soap'. (*Geoffrey Barnsley*)

A Ladymoor scene showing Joe Richards outside his terrace home talking to his niece Gloria, who is just discernible through the windscreen of the motorbike. The view is looking towards the village centre, with the Brickmakers Arms on the left, *c.* 1958. (*Joe Richards*)

It was at this point in Ladymoor that the old road from Bilston to Coseley emerged, before the present newer road was constructed during the last quarter of the eighteenth century. The background of course shows the steelworks; nearer, we see the old ford. Collins' shop, seen on the left, did a good trade in sweets owing to the school which lay opposite. The hutmen was long Ruby Cotterill's fish and chips shop and the cot part-seen on the right was the home of Tom France. (*Author*)

A week after this photograph was taken in 2002 Ladymoor School was no more, a sad day. The buildings, though never extensive, were architecturally a pleasant feature of the area. The tall windows and the roof dormers gave the school buildings considerable interest. This was the school that encouraged and produced some fine artists, such as Robert Baker, Andrew Barnett and Harry Eccleston. (*Author*)

Before the Second World War, a new annexe was built in the school grounds for the purpose of domestic science for the girls and woodwork for the boys. Here, on a special open day for parents in the mid-1950s, Geoffrey Barnsley proudly shows some of his work to his father, Mr Colin Barnsley. (*Geoffrey Barnsley*)

A holiday venue for the pupils of Ladymoor School was the ancestral home of the Marquis of Anglesey. The house, known as Beaudesert, lies on the south-east tip of Cannock Chase. Seen enjoying the day are, from left to right, Ken Lowe, Mr Hart, -?-, Sally Turton, Miss Giles and Geoffrey Barnsley. They were supposed to be working, collecting firewood! (*Geoffrey Barnsley*)

Another view of Beaudesert, where in this vast landscape the Ladymoor School football team happily pose for the camera, *c.* 1948. Seen here, back row third from the left in a goalie sweater, is Geoffrey Barnsley, and front row centre is Jim Lavender. Geoffrey for some time played football for West Bromwich Albion, Plymouth Argyll and Norwich. (*Geoffrey Barnsley*)

The Ladymoor School 1st XI football team posing this time in the school playground, autumn 1950. Back row, left to right: B. Ball, L. Parker, G. Barnsley (vice-captain), S. Pearson (captain), W. Gittings, A. Mansfield. Front row: H. Webb, T. Bell, D. Evans, E. Hayden, J. Lavender. (*A. Wilkes & Son. Donated by Gwen Lang*)

Three old Ladymoor School scholars meet up at a school reunion. The man on the left is unknown, centre is Ray Richards and right is Arthur Wootton, *c.* 1995. (*Arthur Wootton*)

Lads from Ladymoor and Daisy Bank enjoy an independent camping holiday at the Bratch, Wombourne, 1934. Left to right, -?-, -?-, Alfred Baker, ? Crudgington, Howard Dainty, Harry Eccleston (chopping firewood), -?-, -?-.

A winter scene at Ladymoor Pool. (*Gwen Lang*)

The mess at the side of Ladymoor Pool was where the new Black Country Route was scheduled to go, until a change of plan favoured its present situation closer to Bilston town. What they are laying here in about 1980 are huge sewer mains. The Ladymoor Infants School is seen on the right and part of the vast steelworks tipping area is seen in the background. (*Author*)

This sketch shows how the area of Ladymoor Pool once looked, *c.* 1940. The path led from Highfields Road between the pool and the brook (which carried surplus water away from the Deepfields Drainer) to Darkhouse Chapel. The distant embankment carried the canal, over which can be seen the Blue Button footbridge; the hill to the right was spoil from Blue Button Colliery. The ridges seen at the foot of the embankment were probably the last remnants of the medieval ridge and furrow method of agriculture in the Black Country. The chain fencing in the foreground was once part of the rattle-chain system from the engine to the pit shaft, to lower and raise the cages. (*Author*)

The Deepfields Drainer, or the Five Boilers as it was locally known, *c.* 1925. It dominated the Ladymoor area with its stacks and pumping engine buildings, and the boilers which lay at the foot of the largest stack. The task of the drainer was to ensure the local coal pits were kept dry. The whole has long since disappeared, but the well still remains and is regularly checked for water levels. In the right foreground there is a sluice point, much the same as those seen working canal locks. (*Author*)

The view towards Ladymoor from Highfields (Boat) Bridge, *c.* 1980. The old houses nos 46 to 56 were demolished in about 1984 to allow for bridge and road improvements here. (*Author*)

Almost from the same spot near the Boat Bridge, on the open land (now afforested) looking north, there lies what was known as Ramsbottom's Pool. It was once an idyllic spot, but in the area during the last war an unexploded German bomb was discovered. Capponfield House is seen reflected in the water, the Broadmoor housing estate lies to the left of the picture and Capponfield works to the right. This is a mid-1970s photograph. (*Author*)

This scene inside the West Bromwich Albion changing room shows football ace Len Millard (left) giving some friendly advice to up-and-coming goalkeeper Geoff Barnsley, 22 January 1955. (*Gwen Lang*)

ACKNOWLEDGEMENTS

Thanks to: Betty Aston, John Aston, Reg Aston, Robert Baker, Geoffrey Barnsley, Ray Barnsley, Annette Beaton, Brenda C. Beech, Jack Braddock, Norma Bradley, Bob Cartwright, Iris Clarke, Ray Clarke, British Coal, Anita Cooper, Ken Cooper, Lyn Cooper, Joan Davies, Gavin Dickson, Harold Dugmore, Harry N. Eccleston OBE, Alan Evans, Maisie Evans, Ken Fellows, Margaret Flavell, Jon George, Vi Grainger, Samuel Griffiths, Bill Grinsell, Becky Gripton, John Guest, Bob Hampton, Margaret Hampton, Roy Hawthorne, Iris Hazlehurst, Stan Hill, Remi Hodister, Bryan Hollies, Harold Humphries, Harry Johnson, Emily Kinsey, Joe Knight, Ann Lakin, Gwen Lang, Marjorie Martin, Edward Matthews Ltd, L. McGowen, Eric Morley, Joan Moseley, Robert Noyes, Ivor Palmer, Ron Perry, Judy Polkinhorn, Bill Price, John Price (printers), Kath Price, Beryl Pugh, Eric Pugh, Doreen Pye, Eileen Reynolds, Joe Richards, Joan Rickuss, Polly Shepherd, Derek Simpkiss, Joyce Sinclair, Jack Smith, George Stevens, Myra Thompson, Dennis Turner MP, Revd Richard Walker, N. Wilkinson, Judy Wilson, Derek Wood, Gary Woodberry and Arthur Wootton. Further acknowledgements are due to the Black Country Society, staff of Bilston Library, Wolverhampton *Express and Star*, Bennett and Clark (photographers), Bradley Medical Centre, Dr C. Lal and Cole's Furnishers. The author is most grateful to everyone who has loaned or donated photographs either in the past or specifically for this book, with special thanks to all anonymous contributors.

Every effort has been made to contact copyright holders of photographs where this has not originated with the person owning them. All royalties from this book are to be donated to Compton Hospice.